THE SLIM 800 HOT AIR FRYER
Recipe Cookbook

THE SLIM 800 HOT AIR FRYER RECIPE COOKBOOK

DELICIOUS & SIMPLE MEALS FOR YOUR HOT AIR FRYER

ISBN 978-1-913005-49-8

DISCLAIMER

Except for use in any review, the reproduction or utilisation of this work in whole or in part in any form by any electronic, mechanical or other means, now known or hereafter invented, including xerography, photocopying and recording, or in any information storage or retrieval system, is forbidden without the permission of the publisher.

This book is sold subject to the condition that it shall not, by way of trade or otherwise, be lent, resold, hired out or otherwise circulated without the prior consent of the publisher in any form of binding or cover other than that in which it is published and without a similar condition including this condition being imposed on the subsequent purchaser.

This book is designed to provide information on meals, snacks & desserts that can be made using an electric hot air fryer appliance. Some recipes may contain nuts or traces of nuts. Those suffering from any allergies associated with nuts should avoid any recipes containing nuts or nut based oils. This information is provided and sold with the knowledge that the publisher and author do not offer any legal or other professional advice. In the case of a need for any such expertise consult with the appropriate professional.

This book does not contain all information available on the subject, and other sources of recipes are available.
Every effort has been made to make this book as accurate as possible. However, there may be typographical and or content errors. Therefore, this book should serve only as a general guide and not as the ultimate source of subject information.

This book contains information that might be dated and is intended only to educate and entertain. The author and publisher shall have no liability or responsibility to any person or entity regarding any loss or damage incurred, or alleged to have incurred, directly or indirectly, by the information contained in this book.

CONTENTS

INTRODUCTION	6
STARTERS	**11**
Fresh Tortilla Chips	12
Paprika Onion Rings	13
Mini Pepper Poppers	14
Cheese Pearls	15
Fried Cornichons	16
Sesame Tofu Cubes	17
Bitesize Meatballs	18
Turkey Scotch Eggs	19
Sweet Chilli Chicken Wings	20
Mustard Chicken Strips	21
Avocado Spring Rolls	22
Rosemary Potato Chips	23
Crispy Garlic Kale Chips	24
Roasted Curry Cauli	25
Almond Potato Chips	26
Honey Chestnuts	27
Vegetable Egg Rolls	28
Chicken Parmesan Bites	29
Halloumi Mushrooms	30
Spicy Calamari	31
Breaded Button Mushrooms	32
Avocado Fingers	33
Pancetta & Cheese Bites	34
Loose Onion Bhajis	35
Spicy Whole Prawns	36

MAIN COURSE DISHES - MEAT & POULTRY — 37

Parmesan Chicken Strips	38
Straight-Up Fried Drummers	39
Pesto Chicken Breasts	40
Perfect Whole Chicken	41
Barbeque Whole Chicken	42
Lemon Chicken Wings	43
Mozzarella Chicken	44
Chicken Puff Tarts	45
Marrakech Chicken Goujons & Dip	46
Sliced 'Fried' Hog	47
Mozzarella Beef Burgers	48
Spanish Stuffed Pork Tenderloin	49
Mustard Stuffed Sausages	50
Cracked Pepper Steak	51
Honey Mustard Pork Chops	52
Lamb Kofta	53
Rosemary Lamb Chops	54

MAIN COURSE DISHES - FISH & SEAFOOD — 55

Tuna Croquettes	56
Dusted Lemon Sole Fillets	57
Tortilla Fried Fish	58
Sweet Chilli Salmon	59
Thai Crab Cakes	60
Balsamic Tuna Steaks	61
Crab Rolls	62

MAIN COURSE DISHES - VEGETABLES — 63

Feta Filo Pies	64
Pesto & Tomato Tarts	65
Pine Nut Topped Tomatoes	66
Ricotta Stuffed Mushrooms	67
Aubergine Ciabatta	68

VEGETABLE SIDES — 69

Nutmeg Roasted Turnip	70
Parmesan Mini Corn	71
Crunchy Coated Sprouts	72
Fried Garlic Asparagus	73
Courgette Basil Buttons	74
Skinny Sweet Potato Fries	75
Crunchy Parmesan Sweet Potato Fries	76
Sweet Potato Coconut Dumplings	77
Sweet Parmentier	78
Roast Salad Potatoes	79
Chips Chips Chips	80
Herbed Wedges	81
Patatas Bravas	82
Broccoli & Potato Croquettes	83
Soured Cream Baked Potatoes	84

DESSERTS — 85

The Easiest Apple Turnovers Ever	86
Cookie Puffs	87
Chocolate Roti	88
Banana Gyoza Dumplings	89
Blueberry Strudel	90
Cinnamon Pears	91
Fried Panko Bananas	92

INTRODUCTION

What Is the Slim '800' Lifestyle?

The Slim 800 Diet is an effort to return to a healthier way of eating that emphasizes fasting and balanced nutrition.

Fasting is probably most well-known as the 5:2 Diet - a great and flexible way to approach weight loss and less restrictive than many other diets. The 5:2 approach means you can eat 'normally' for 5 days a week and fast for 2. It's revolutionised the way people think about dieting.

By allowing you the freedom to eat normally for MOST of the week and fast by restricting your calorie intake for just TWO non-consecutive days a week (800 calories per day for men and women), you keep yourself motivated and remove that dreaded feeling of constantly denying yourself the food you really want to eat. It still takes willpower, but it's nowhere near as much of a grind when you know that you have tomorrow to look forward to. It's all about freedom. The ability to be flexible with the days you choose to fast makes the likelihood of you sticking to the diet for a prolonged period, or even indefinitely as a lifestyle choice, much higher than a regime that requires calorie restriction every single day.

With this book we've given you lots of air fryer recipe ideas which you'll be able to use on your fast days and on your 'normal' days. Everything is calorie counted with nutritional breakdown so you'll be able to keep things on track more easily.

Your ultimate guide to healthier frying.

Hot air fryers are revolutionising the way we cook, becoming an indispensable addition to the modern kitchen. Once you experience the convenience and health benefits of a hot air fryer, you'll wonder how you ever lived without one!

A hot air fryer allows you to create quick, easy, and healthy meals with just a fraction of the oil required by traditional frying methods. There's no need for preheating or mixing, and it can cook a wide variety of dishes, from snacks to main courses—not just chips! Speaking of which, air-fried chips deserve a special mention for their crispy perfection achieved with minimal oil, making them a healthier option.

The Slim 800 Hot Air Fryer Recipe Cookbook: Delicious & Simple Meals For Your Hot Air Fryer is your ultimate guide to healthier frying. It features a diverse collection of recipes, including starters, main courses, sides, and desserts. Whether you're preparing a family meal, hosting a party, or indulging in a snack, this cookbook has you covered. It's the only hot air fryer recipe book you'll ever need!

HOW DOES HOT AIR FRYING WORK?

Unlike traditional deep frying, a hot air fryer uses very hot air (up to 200°C) to circulate around the food, cooking it quickly with a crispy outer layer.

TEMPERATURE CONTROL

Most air fryers come with adjustable temperature controls and timers. If yours doesn't, it's likely preset to cook at 200°C/400°F. Keep an eye on cooking times to ensure perfect results.

HOW CAN IT FRY WITH SO LITTLE OIL?

The efficient hot air circulation requires only a minimal amount of oil. Often, a light spray of oil is enough, making it the healthiest way to fry. Choose your preferred low calorie spray oil, whether it's olive, coconut, or sunflower oil.

> *We use fresh, inexpensive, lower-calorie and lower-fat ingredients, all readily available at your local supermarket.*

DOES HOT AIR FRIED FRIED FOOD TASTE DIFFERENT?

Hot air fried food often tastes better than traditional fried food. The reduced fat content doesn't compromise flavour, and the method preserves the natural taste of your ingredients.

CLEANER, SAFER, HEALTHIER

Hot air fryers use significantly less oil—often just a spoonful—making them a healthier option compared to traditional deep fryers. They use fresh oil for each cooking session, eliminating strong odours and smoke. This method is not only healthier but also safer, with most fryers pausing the cooking process when the lid is lifted.

OUR RECIPES

Reflecting the simplicity of hot air frying, our recipes are easy to follow with minimal preparation and cooking times. We use fresh, inexpensive, lower-calorie and lower-fat ingredients, all readily available at your local supermarket. Each recipe includes calorie counts and nutritional information, perfect for those following an 800-calorie fasting day. We minimise the use of store cupboard ingredients to keep your store cupboard streamlined and your cooking affordable. Some recipes serve four, and given that air fryer capacities vary, you might need to adjust cooking times for batch cooking.

TIPS

To get the best results from your hot air fryer, keep these tips in mind:

- Remove food promptly once cooking is complete to maintain crispiness.
- Clean your appliance after each use; most parts are dishwasher safe.
- Avoid abrasive cleaning materials to protect the non-stick coating.
- Ensure food has plenty of space in the fryer for even cooking.
- Read the manufacturer's instructions thoroughly to understand your fryer's functions and maintain the warranty.
- Air fryers vary in capacity; you may need to cook in batches.
- Preheat your air fryer before adding food.
- Cooking times are guidelines; check your food to ensure it's thoroughly cooked before serving.

Once you experience the convenience and health benefits of a hot air fryer, you'll wonder how you ever lived without one!

STARTERS

FRESH TORTILLA CHIPS

Serves 4

INGREDIENTS

- 8 fresh wholewheat tortilla wraps
- Low calorie spray oil
- Crushed sea salt flakes

NUTRITION

- Calories: 260
- Protein: 6g
- Total Fat: 6g
- Saturated Fat: 2g
- Carbs: 42g
- Fibre: 4g
- Sugars: 2g

METHOD

1 Pile four wraps on top of each other and cut into 8 equal wedges (to make 32 chips). Do the same with the next four wraps.

2 Spray each wedge well on each side with oil and place in the air fryer basket.

3 Cook for approx. 8-10 minutes on 400f/200C. Open up the fryer now and again during cooking and give the basket a good shake.

4 Cook only half the chips at a time to ensure even cooking. Sprinkle with the sea salt flakes and serve.

GREAT FOR NACHOS

PAPRIKA ONION RINGS

Serves 4

INGREDIENTS

- 200g/7oz wholegrain crackers
- 125g/4oz plain flour
- 1 tsp salt
- 1 tbsp paprika
- 3 large white onions
- 250ml/1 cup low fat buttermilk
- 1 egg
- Low calorie spray oil

NUTRITION

- Calories: 425
- Protein: 13g
- Total Fat: 9g
- Saturated Fat: 2.5g
- Carbs: 70g
- Fibre: 6g
- Sugars: 10.5g

METHOD

1 First whizz the wholegrain crackers, flour, salt & paprika in a food processor to make fine breadcrumbs. When ready, tip into a shallow dish.

2 Peel and cut the onions into thick rings.

3 Beat the egg and buttermilk in a bowl.

4 Lay some baking parchment on a baking tray.

5 Dip each ring into the beaten egg then press it in the breadcrumbs to fully coat it. When it's well covered place on the baking parchment.

6 Spray each ring well with oil and place in the air fryer basket.

7 Cook for approx. 8-10 minutes on 400f/200C. Turn once halfway through cooking and spray with additional oil.

8 Don't put too many rings in at a time. Give them plenty of room in the basket and cook in batches of 4-6 if necessary.

MINI PEPPER POPPERS

Serves 4

INGREDIENTS

- 8 slices turkey bacon
- 16 mini sweet peppers
- 175g/6oz low fat soft cream cheese
- Wooden cocktail sticks
- Low calorie spray oil

NUTRITION

- Calories: 196
- Protein: 12g
- Total Fat: 12g
- Saturated Fat: 6g
- Carbs: 10g
- Fibre: 2g
- Sugars: 7g

METHOD

1 Cut each bacon slice in half lengthways to make 16 lengths.

2 Make a slit down one side of each pepper and carefully de-seed.

3 Fill each pepper with a teaspoon of two of the cream cheese. Wrap a length of bacon tightly around each pepper and spear in place with a cocktail stick.

4 Spray each prepared pepper well with oil and place in the air fryer basket. Cook for approx. 15 minutes on 400f/200C, turning once halfway through cooking.

5 Don't put too many peppers in at a time. Give them plenty of room in the basket and cook in batches of 6-8 if necessary until the bacon is cooked and the cream cheese is piping hot.

PERFECT FOR PARTIES

CHEESE PEARLS

Serves 4

INGREDIENTS

- 3 tbsp cornstarch
- Pinch of salt
- 200g/7oz wholewheat breadcrumbs
- 1 tbsp dried mixed herbs
- 1 tsp chilli flakes
- 2 eggs
- 250g/9oz low fat mozzarella pearls
- Low calorie spray oil

NUTRITION

- Calories: 392
- Protein: 23g
- Total Fat: 15g
- Saturated Fat: 7g
- Carbs: 42g
- Fibre: 2.5g
- Sugars: 4g

METHOD

1 Add the cornstarch and salt to a plastic bag.

2 Combine together the breadcrumbs, herbs and chilli in bowl.

3 Beat the eggs together in a separate bowl

4 Lay some baking parchment on a plate on the worktop.

5 Add the cheese to the cornstarch and shake well to fully coat the balls.

6 Dip each ball into the beaten egg then roll it in the breadcrumbs and place on the baking parchment.

7 Spray each ball well with oil and place in the air fryer basket.

8 Cook for approx. 10 minutes on 400f/200C, turning once halfway through cooking.

9 Don't put too many balls in at a time. Give them plenty of room in the basket and cook in batches of 6-8 if necessary.

FRIED CORNICHONS

Serves 4

INGREDIENTS

- 300g/11oz cornichons
- 200g/7oz wholegrain crackers
- 125g/4oz plain flour
- 2 tsp salt
- 2 tsp garlic powder
- 250ml/1 cup low fat buttermilk
- 1 egg
- Low calorie spray oil

NUTRITION

- Calories: 348
- Protein: 12g
- Total Fat: 9g
- Saturated Fat: 2g
- Carbs: 59g
- Fibre: 6g
- Sugars: 6g

METHOD

1 Drain the cornichons and pat dry with kitchen roll.

2 Whizz the wholegrain crackers, flour, salt & garlic in a food processor to make fine breadcrumbs. When ready, tip into a shallow dish.

3 Beat the egg and buttermilk in a bowl. Lay some baking parchment on a baking tray.

4 Tip the cornichons into the beaten egg. Use a slotted spoon to fish them out and roll them in the breadcrumbs to coat them with completely.

5 Place the covered cornichons on the baking parchment. Spray well with oil and place in the air fryer basket.

6 Cook for approx. 8-10 minutes on 400f/200C. Turn once halfway through cooking and spray with a little additional oil. Cook in two batches to ensure even cooking.

SESAME TOFU CUBES

Serves 4

INGREDIENTS

- 1 block tofu (350g/12oz)
- 2 tbsp soy sauce
- 1 tsp sesame oil
- 1 tsp rice vinegar
- 2 tbsp cornstarch
- Low calorie spray oil

NUTRITION

- Calories: 101
- Protein: 9g
- Total Fat: 5g
- Saturated Fat: 1g
- Carbs: 6g
- Fibre: 1g
- Sugars: 1g

METHOD

1 Cut the tofu into bite sized cubes. Combine in a bowl with the soy sauce, sesame oil and rice vinegar and leave to marinate for 10-15 minutes in the fridge.

2 Add the cornstarch to a plastic bag. Add the tofu to the cornstarch and shake well to fully coat the cubes.

3 Spray each cube well with oil and place in the air fryer basket.

4 Cook for approx. 15-20 minutes on 375f/190C. Open up the fryer now and again during cooking and give the basket a good shake.

CHEAP TO MAKE!

BITESIZE MEATBALLS

Serves 4

INGREDIENTS

- 150g/5oz wholegrain breadcrumbs
- 2 eggs, beaten
- 750g/1lb 9oz lean beef mince
- 3 shallots, chopped
- 2 garlic clove, crushed
- ½ tsp salt
- 2 tsp dried mixed herbs
- Low calorie spray oil

NUTRITION

- Calories: 438
- Protein: 38g
- Total Fat: 17g
- Saturated Fat: 6g
- Carbs: 30g
- Fibre: 4g
- Sugars: 4g

METHOD

1 Lay some baking parchment on a baking tray.

2 In a large bowl mix together the breadcrumbs, eggs, mince, shallots, garlic, salt & herbs. Use your hands to really combine the ingredients well.

3 Form into small walnut sized balls and place on the baking parchment.

4 Spray each ball well with oil and place in the air fryer basket.

5 Cook for approx. 10-12 minutes on 375f/190C. Open up the fryer now and again during cooking and give the basket a good shake.

6 Don't put too many meatballs in at a time. Give them plenty of room in the basket and cook in batches of 8-10 if necessary.

TURKEY SCOTCH EGGS

Serves 4

INGREDIENTS

- 450g/1lb Lean turkey mince
- 4 hard boiled eggs, peeled
- 50g/2oz plain flour
- 1 egg, beaten
- 200g/7oz panko breadcrumbs
- 1 tsp salt
- 1 tsp paprika
- Low calorie spray oil

NUTRITION

- Calories: 487
- Protein: 35g
- Total Fat: 17g
- Saturated Fat: 5g
- Carbs: 47g
- Fibre: 3g
- Sugars: 2.5g

METHOD

1 Use a fork to separate the mince.

2 Bring the mince together into 4 firm balls, place these on some baking parchment then flatten each out into a large disc.

3 Roll the peeled eggs in the flour and sit each egg onto a mince disc. Wrap the disc around the egg so that the egg is covered.

4 Dip each mince egg into the beaten egg and roll in the panko breadcrumbs.

5 Spray each ball well with oil and place in the air fryer basket.

6 Cook for approx. 10-12 minutes on 400f/200C. Gently turn once halfway through cooking and spray with additional oil.

SWEET CHILLI CHICKEN WINGS

Serves 4

INGREDIENTS

- 16 small chicken wings
- 1 tbsp baking powder
- 1 tbsp olive oil
- 4 tbsp reduced sugar sweet chilli sauce
- Low calorie spray oil

NUTRITION

- Calories: 485
- Protein: 40g
- Total Fat: 34g
- Saturated Fat: 8.5g
- Carbs: 6g
- Fibre: 0g
- Sugars: 3g

METHOD

1 Dust the chicken wings with baking powder.

2 Spray each wing well with oil and place in the air fryer basket.

3 Cook for 10 minutes on 400f/200C.

4 Whilst the chicken is cooking. Combine together the olive oil and sweet chilli sauce. After the 10 minutes of cooking time is over, brush the chicken with the sweet chilli sauce and oil.

5 Return the wings back to the fryer for approx. 15 minutes or until the wings are cooked through and piping hot.

MUSTARD CHICKEN STRIPS

Serves 4

INGREDIENTS

- 2 large skinless chicken breasts
- 3 tbsp cornstarch
- Pinch of salt
- 1 tsp mustard powder
- 1 tsp garlic powder
- 200g/7oz wholewheat breadcrumbs
- 2 eggs, beaten
- Low calorie spray oil

NUTRITION

- Calories: 347
- Protein: 32g
- Total Fat: 6g
- Saturated Fat: 1.5g
- Carbs: 40g
- Fibre: 3g
- Sugars: 2g

METHOD

1 Cut the chicken into thick finger size strips.

2 Add the cornstarch, salt, mustard powder & garlic powder to a plastic bag.

3 Place the breadcrumbs in a shallow dish and lay some baking parchment on a plate on the worktop.

4 Add the chicken strips to the plastic bag and shake well to fully coat.

5 Dip each strip into the beaten egg then roll it in the breadcrumbs and place on the baking parchment.

6 Spray each strip well with oil and place in the air fryer basket.

7 Cook for approx. 15 minutes on 400f/200C, turning once halfway through cooking.

8 Don't put too many strips in at a time. Give them plenty of room in the basket and cook in batches if necessary.

AVOCADO SPRING ROLLS

Serves 4

INGREDIENTS

- 1 avocado
- 2 tbsp freshly chopped coriander
- 4 vine ripened tomatoes, finely chopped
- 4 shallots, finely chopped
- 1 cucumber, julienned
- 1 tbsp lime juice
- ½ tsp salt
- 8-10 spring roll wrappers
- Low calorie spray oil

NUTRITION

- Calories: 265
- Protein: 6g
- Total Fat: 7g
- Saturated Fat: 1g
- Carbs: 47g
- Fibre: 7g
- Sugars: 8g

METHOD

1 De-stone the avocado and use the back of a fork to gently mash the flesh.

2 Combine together the avocado with the chopped coriander, tomatoes, shallots, cucumber, lime juice and salt.

3 Place a spoonful of avocado mixture in the centre of each wrapper. Bring the bottom edge of the wrapper tightly over the filling, folding in the sides. Continue rolling until the top of the wrapper is reached.

4 Brush the edges of the wrapper with water, pressing to seal. Repeat until all the wrappers are used. (You'll need to experiment with how much mixture to use as you don't want to overfill or under-fill the rolls).

5 Spray each roll well with oil and place in the air fryer basket.

6 Cook for approx. 8-10 minutes on 400f/200C. Turn once halfway through cooking and spray with additional oil.

7 Don't put too many rolls in at a time. Give them plenty of room in the basket and cook in batches of 4 if necessary.

ROSEMARY POTATO CHIPS

Serves 4

INGREDIENTS

- 4 medium Desiree potatoes, unpeeled
- Low calorie spray oil
- 2 tsp fresh rosemary
- Crushed sea salt flakes

NUTRITION

- Calories: 165
- Protein: 4g
- Total Fat: 0g
- Saturated Fat: 0g
- Carbs: 36g
- Fibre: 5g
- Sugars: 2g

METHOD

1 Halve the potatoes lengthways, cut them into very fine slices and pat dry with paper towels.

2 Spray each chip on both sides with oil and place in the air fryer basket.

3 Cook for approx. 15-20 minutes on 400f/200C or until crispy and cooked through. Open up the fryer now and again during cooking and give the basket a good shake.

4 Cook only half the chips at a time to ensure even cooking.

5 Toss the chips with the sea salt flakes and rosemary and serve.

CRISPY GARLIC KALE CHIPS

Serves 4

INGREDIENTS

- 200g/7oz kale
- 1 tbsp olive oil
- 2 tsp garlic powder
- Crushed sea salt flakes
- Low calorie spray oil

NUTRITION

- Calories: 60
- Protein: 2g
- Total Fat: 4g
- Saturated Fat: 0.5g
- Carbs: 6g
- Fibre: 2g
- Sugars: 1g

METHOD

1 In a bowl combine together the kale, olive oil, garlic powder and salt.

2 Cook for approx. 10-14 minutes on 400f/200C or until the kale is crispy and cooked through. Open up the fryer now and again during cooking to give the basket a good shake and spray a little more oil.

3 Cook only half the kale at a time to ensure even cooking.

4 Toss the chips with the sea salt flakes and rosemary and serve.

ROASTED CURRY CAULI

Serves 4

INGREDIENTS

- 1 cauliflower head
- 1 tbsp olive oil
- 1 tsp garlic powder
- 1 tbsp curry powder
- Crushed sea salt flakes
- Low calorie spray oil

NUTRITION

- Calories: 88
- Protein: 4g
- Total Fat: 4g
- Saturated Fat: 0.5g
- Carbs: 11g
- Fibre: 4.5g
- Sugars: 3.5g

METHOD

1 Carefully break the cauliflower head up into really small pieces.

2 In a bowl combine together the cauliflower, olive oil, garlic powder, curry powder & salt.

3 Cook for approx. 15-20 minutes on 400f/200C or until the cauliflower is tender and cooked through.

4 Open up the fryer now and again during cooking to give the basket a good shake and spray a little more oil.

ALMOND POTATO CHIPS

Serves 4

INGREDIENTS

- 4 medium Desiree potatoes, unpeeled
- Low calorie spray oil
- 4 tbsp ground almonds
- Crushed sea salt flakes

NUTRITION

- Calories: 204
- Protein: 6g
- Total Fat: 4g
- Saturated Fat: 0.25g
- Carbs: 38g
- Fibre: 6g
- Sugars: 2g

METHOD

1 Halve the potatoes lengthways, cut into very fine slices and pat dry with paper towels.

2 Sprinkle the ground almonds over the chops and spray on both sides with oil.

3 Place in the air fryer basket and cook for approx. 15-20 minutes on 400f/200C or until crispy and cooked through. Open up the fryer now and again during cooking and give the basket a good shake.

4 Cook only half the chips at a time to ensure even cooking.

DELICIOUS

HONEY CHESTNUTS

Serves 4

INGREDIENTS

- 400g/14oz chestnuts
- 2 tbsp honey
- 1 tbsp olive oil
- Low calorie spray oil

NUTRITION

- Calories: 240
- Protein: 2g
- Total Fat: 4g
- Saturated Fat: 0.75g
- Carbs: 49g
- Fibre: 7g
- Sugars: 17.5g

METHOD

1 Use a knife to cut a small cross in the top each chestnut. Leave to soak in cold water for half an hour.

2 Dry with kitchen paper, spray with the oil, place in the air fryer basket and cook for approx. 10 minutes on 375f/190C.

3 Remove from the fryer and place in a bowl with the honey and olive oil. Combine well, return the nuts to the fryer basket and continue to cook to for a further 10 minutes or until the chestnuts are tender and cooked through.

4 Peel the brown outer skin and enjoy the soft cooked nut inside.

VEGETABLE EGG ROLLS

Serves 4

INGREDIENTS

- 1 stalk celery, sliced into thin strips
- 1 small carrot, sliced into thin strips
- 75g/3oz beansprouts
- Handful of button mushrooms, finely diced
- ½ tsp freshly grated ginger
- 1 tsp sugar
- 1 tsp vegetable stock powder
- 8-10 spring roll wrappers
- Low calorie spray oil

NUTRITION

- Calories: 169
- Protein: 4g
- Total Fat: 1g
- Saturated Fat: 0g
- Carbs: 36g
- Fibre: 2g
- Sugars: 3.5g

METHOD

1 To make the spring roll filling combine together the celery, carrots, beansprouts, mushrooms, ginger, sugar stock powder and stir evenly.

2 Place a spoonful of the filling in the centre of each wrapper. Bring the bottom edge of the wrapper tightly over the filling, folding in the sides. Continue rolling until the top of the wrapper is reached.

3 Brush the edges of the wrapper with water, pressing to seal. Repeat until all the wrappers are used. (You'll need to experiment with how much filling to use as you don't want to overfill or under-fill the rolls).

4 Spray each roll well with oil and place in the air fryer basket.

5 Cook for approx. 8-10 minutes on 400f/200C. Turn once halfway through cooking and spray with additional oil.

6 Don't put too many rolls in at a time. Give them plenty of room in the basket and cook in batches of 4 if necessary.

CHICKEN PARMESAN BITES

Serves 4

INGREDIENTS

- 2 chicken breasts, cubed into bite size chunks
- 3 tbsp cornstarch
- Pinch of salt
- 200g/7oz breadcrumbs
- 1 tbsp mixed dried herbs
- 2 tbsp grated Parmesan cheese
- 2 eggs
- Low calorie spray oil

NUTRITION

- Calories: 246
- Protein: 10g
- Total Fat: 5g
- Saturated Fat: 2g
- Carbs: 43g
- Fibre: 2g
- Sugars: 3g

METHOD

1 Add the cornstarch and salt to a plastic bag.

2 Combine together the breadcrumbs, herbs and Parmesan in bowl.

3 Beat the eggs together in a separate bowl

4 Lay some baking parchment on a plate on the worktop.

5 Add the cubed chicken to the cornstarch and shake well to fully coat.

6 Dip each chicken bite into the beaten egg then roll it in the breadcrumbs and place on the baking parchment.

7 Spray each bite well with oil and place in the air fryer basket.

8 Cook for approx. 15-20 minutes on 350f/175C. Turn once halfway through cooking and spray with additional oil. Ensure the chicken is cooked through and piping hot.

9 Don't put too many bites in at a time. Give them plenty of room in the basket and cook in batches of 6-8 if necessary.

HALLOUMI MUSHROOMS

Serves 4

INGREDIENTS

- 4 large flat mushrooms
- 2 cloves garlic, crushed
- 1 large beef tomato, diced
- 225g/8oz halloumi cheese, diced
- 2 tbsp reduced sugar sweet chilli sauce
- Low calorie spray oil

NUTRITION

- Calories: 245
- Protein: 16g
- Total Fat: 16g
- Saturated Fat: 11g
- Carbs: 11g
- Fibre: 1.5g
- Sugars: 6g

METHOD

1 Combine together the garlic, tomatoes, cheese and chilli sauce.

2 Load the cheese mixture evenly onto the underside of the mushrooms

3 Spray each mushroom well all over with oil and place in the air fryer basket.

4 Cook for approx. 10-15 minutes on 350f/175C or until the mushrooms are cooked through and the cheese is bubbling and piping hot.

5 Don't put too many mushrooms in at a time. Give them plenty of room in the basket and cook in batches if necessary.

SPICY CALAMARI

Serves 4

INGREDIENTS

- 200g/7oz water biscuits
- 3 tbsp plain flour
- 1 tsp salt
- 1 tsp crushed chilli
- 250g/1lb squid rings
- 250ml/1 cup low fat buttermilk
- 1 egg
- Low calorie spray oil

NUTRITION

- Calories: 359
- Protein: 17g
- Total Fat: 8g
- Saturated Fat: 3.5g
- Carbs: 50g
- Fibre: 2g
- Sugars: 6g

METHOD

1 First whizz the water biscuits, flour, salt & chilli in a food processor to make fine breadcrumbs. When ready, tip into a shallow dish.

2 Dry off the squid rings with kitchen roll.

3 Beat the egg and buttermilk in a bowl.

4 Lay some baking parchment on a baking tray.

5 Dip each ring into the beaten egg then press it in the breadcrumbs to fully coat it. When it's well covered place on the baking parchment.

6 Spray each ring well with oil and place in the air fryer basket.

7 Cook for approx. 10-14 minutes on 400f/200C. Turn once halfway through cooking and spray with additional oil.

8 Don't put too many rings in at a time. Give them plenty of room in the basket and cook in batches of 4-6 if necessary.

BREADED BUTTON MUSHROOMS

Serves 4

INGREDIENTS

- 2 tsp garlic powder
- 200g/7oz panko breadcrumbs
- 250g/9oz button mushrooms
- 2 cloves garlic, peeled and chopped
- 50g/2oz plain flour
- 1 egg, beaten
- Low calorie spray oil

NUTRITION

- Calories: 268
- Protein: 10g
- Total Fat: 3g
- Saturated Fat: 0.6g
- Carbs: 50g
- Fibre: 3g
- Sugars: 4g

METHOD

1 Combine together the garlic powder and breadcrumbs in a bowl.

2 Dip each mushroom into the beaten egg and roll in the garlic panko breadcrumbs.

3 Spray each mushroom well with oil, place in the air fryer basket and cook for approx. 5-7 minutes on 400f/200C.

4 Don't put too many mushrooms in at a time. Give them plenty of room in the basket and cook in batches if necessary.

AVOCADO FINGERS

Serves 4

INGREDIENTS

- 2 firm avocados
- 200g/7oz water biscuits
- 125g/4oz plain flour
- 1 tsp salt
- 3 large white onions
- Low calorie spray oil

NUTRITION

- Calories: 534
- Protein: 9g
- Total Fat: 17g
- Saturated Fat: 4g
- Carbs: 83g
- Fibre: 11g
- Sugars: 16g

METHOD

1 First whizz the water biscuits, flour & salt in a food processor to make fine breadcrumbs. When ready tip into a shallow dish.

2 De-stone the avocados and scoop out the flesh. Cut each avocado half into four thick slices.

3 Lay some baking parchment on a baking tray.

4 Gently press the avocado fingers into the breadcrumbs to fully coat them. When completely covered place these onto the baking parchment.

5 Spray each finger well with oil and place in the air fryer basket.

6 Cook for approx. 5-7 minutes on 400f/200C. Shake once halfway through cooking and spray with additional oil.

7 Don't put too many fingers in at a time. Give them plenty of room in the basket and cook in batches if necessary.

PANCETTA & CHEESE BITES

Serves 4

INGREDIENTS

- 450g/1lb mature low fat Cheddar cheese
- 12 pancetta slices
- 50g/2oz wholewheat breadcrumbs
- 60g/2oz plain flour
- 2 eggs, beaten
- Low calorie spray oil

NUTRITION

- Calories: 586
- Protein: 37g
- Total Fat: 27g
- Saturated Fat: 13g
- Carbs: 24g
- Fibre: 1g
- Sugars: 0.5g

METHOD

1 Cut the Cheddar cheese block into 12 equal cubes. Wrap pancetta around each piece of cheddar, fully enclosing the cheese and put them in the freezer for 5 minutes to firm, and then remove.

2 Dip each pancetta cube into the flour, then the eggs and then the breadcrumbs, pressing to ensure the coating sticks.

3 Spray each cube well with oil and place in the air fryer basket.

4 Cook for approx. 8-10 minutes on 400f/200C. Turn once halfway through cooking and spray with additional oil.

5 Don't put too many cubes in at a time. Give them plenty of room in the basket and cook in batches if necessary.

LOOSE ONION BHAJIS

Serves 4

INGREDIENTS

- 4 onions, peeled & diced
- 2 eggs, beaten
- 125g/4oz plain flour
- 1 tsp ground coriander
- 1 tsp ground powder
- 2 tsp mild curry powder
- Low calorie spray oil

NUTRITION

- Calories: 214
- Protein: 8g
- Total Fat: 3g
- Saturated Fat: 1g
- Carbs: 39g
- Fibre: 5g
- Sugars: 12g

METHOD

1 Combine together the onions, eggs, flour, coriander, cumin and curry and bring together into four balls.

2 Spray each ball well with oil and place in the air fryer basket.

3 Cook for approx. 10-15 minutes on 400f/200C. Turn once halfway through cooking and spray with additional oil.

4 Make sure there is plenty of room for each bhaji in the basket and cook in batches if necessary.

SPICY WHOLE PRAWNS

Serves 4

INGREDIENTS

- 450g/1lb large king prawns
- 1 tsp cornflour
- 1 tsp Tabasco sauce
- 1 tsp chilli flakes
- 1 tsp dried oregano
- ½ tsp dried parsley
- ½ tsp pepper
- ½ tsp garlic powder
- ½ tsp onion salt
- ½ tsp smoked paprika
- Low calorie spray oil

NUTRITION

- Calories: 123
- Protein: 23g
- Total Fat: 1g
- Saturated Fat: 0.25g
- Carbs: 3g
- Fibre: 1g
- Sugars: 0g

METHOD

1 Shell the prawns but leave the tips of their tails on if possible (don't worry if not).

2 Combine together all the ingredients in a plastic bag (except the prawns and low calorie spray oil).

3 Add the prawns and shake the bag well to coat each prawn.

4 Spray each prawn well with oil and place in the air fryer basket. Cook for approx. 6-8 minutes on 400f/200C, turning once halfway through cooking and spring with more oil.

5 Don't put too many prawns in at a time. Give them plenty of room in the basket and cook in batches if necessary.

MAIN COURSES MEAT & POULTRY

PARMESAN CHICKEN STRIPS

Serves 4

INGREDIENTS

- 4 skinless chicken breasts
- 2 tbsp plain flour
- 2 tbsp grated Parmesan
- 100g/3oz panko breadcrumbs
- 2 eggs, beaten
- Low calorie spray oil

NUTRITION

- Calories: 339
- Protein: 42g
- Total Fat: 8g
- Saturated Fat: 2g
- Carbs: 22g
- Fibre: 1g
- Sugars: 1g

METHOD

1 Cut the chicken into thick finger size strips.

2 Add the flour and Parmesan to a plastic bag.

3 Place the breadcrumbs in a shallow dish and lay some baking parchment on a plate on the worktop.

4 Add the chicken strips to the plastic bag and shake well to fully coat.

5 Dip each strip into the beaten egg then roll it in the panko breadcrumbs and place on the baking parchment.

6 Spray each strip well with oil and place in the air fryer basket.

7 Cook for approx. 15 minutes on 400f/200C, turning once halfway through cooking.

8 Don't put too many strips in at a time. Give them plenty of room in the basket and cook in batches if necessary.

STRAIGHT-UP FRIED DRUMMERS

Serves 4

INGREDIENTS

- 60g/2oz self raising flour
- 1 tbsp garlic powder
- 1 tbsp paprika
- 2 tsp salt
- 8 chicken drumsticks
- 3 eggs, beaten
- Low calorie spray oil

NUTRITION

- Calories: 410
- Protein: 39g
- Total Fat: 21g
- Saturated Fat: 6g
- Carbs: 15g
- Fibre: 1g
- Sugars: 0g

METHOD

1 Add the flour, garlic powder, paprika and salt to a plastic bag.

2 Dip the drumsticks in the beaten eggs and add to the flour bag.

3 Shake well to fully coat and place on a tray with some baking parchment. (Don't add more than 3 or 4 chicken pieces at a time)

4 Spray each drumstick well with oil and place in the air fryer basket.

5 Cook for approx. 25-30 minutes on 400f/200C, turning once halfway through cooking and spray with a little more oil.

6 Cook in batches to allow plenty of space in the basket. Ensure the chicken is cooked through and piping hot.

PESTO CHICKEN BREASTS

Serves 4

INGREDIENTS

- 4 small skinless chicken breasts
- 4 tbsp low fat green pesto
- 3 tbsp plain flour
- 100g/3oz panko breadcrumbs
- 2 eggs
- Wooden cocktail sticks
- Low calorie spray oil

NUTRITION

- Calories: 374
- Protein: 41g
- Total Fat: 10g
- Saturated Fat: 2.5g
- Carbs: 25g
- Fibre: 2g
- Sugars: 1.5g

METHOD

1 Butterfly each breast so that it opens out to double its size. Spread a tablespoon of pesto to the inner side and close the breast over back to its original shape (basically you are just spreading pesto through the centre of the chicken).

2 Put the flour on a plate. Place the breadcrumbs in a shallow dish, lay some baking parchment on a plate on the worktop and beat the eggs in a shallow bowl.

3 Gently roll the breasts in the flour. Keeping them closed over so that pesto stays hidden in the centre. Dip each breast into the beaten egg and roll it in the panko breadcrumbs, again keeping the breast intact.

4 Place on the baking parchment and spear each breast with a cocktail stick to hold it together.

5 Spray well with oil and place in the air fryer basket. Cook for approx. 30-35 minutes on 400f/200C. Turn once halfway through cooking and spray with a little more oil. Ensure the chicken is cooked through and piping hot before serving.

6 Give each breast plenty of room in the basket and cook in batches if necessary.

PERFECT WHOLE CHICKEN

Serves 6

INGREDIENTS

- 1 small chicken (choose one which will fit in your device)
- 1 tbsp celery salt
- 2 tsp brown
- 1 tsp paprika
- ½ tsp turmeric
- ½ tsp onion powder
- ½ tsp garlic power
- ½ teaspoon cornstarch
- Low calorie spray oil

NUTRITION

- Calories: 409
- Protein: 40g
- Total Fat: 27g
- Saturated Fat: 8g
- Carbs: 2g
- Fibre: 0g
- Sugars: 1g

METHOD

1 Combine together all the dry ingredients to make a seasoned salt mix.

2 Pat dry the skin of the chicken with kitchen roll and use your hands to rub the seasoned salt all over the bird.

3 Spray well with oil and place in the air fryer basket.

4 Cook for approx. 60-75 minutes on 400f/200C, turning once halfway through cooking and spraying with more oil.

5 Ensure the chicken is cooked through and piping hot before serving.

BARBEQUE WHOLE CHICKEN

Serves 6

INGREDIENTS

- 1 small chicken (choose one which will fit in your device)
- 2 tbsp brown sugar
- 120ml/½ cup ketchup
- 120ml/½ cup water
- ½ tsp salt
- 120ml/½ cup white vinegar
- 1 tsp soy sauce
- 2 cloves garlic, crushed
- Low calorie spray oil

NUTRITION

- Calories: 438
- Protein: 40g
- Total Fat: 27g
- Saturated Fat: 8g
- Carbs: 10g
- Fibre: 0g
- Sugars: 8g

METHOD

1 Combine together the sugar, ketchup, water, salt, vinegar, soy and garlic together to make a sauce.

2 Brush this all over the whole chicken, place the sauce & chicken in a large plastic bag and leave to marinate for a few hours (or overnight) in the fridge, turning occasionally to coat the chicken well.

3 Spray well with oil and place in the air fryer basket.

4 Cook for approx. 60-75 minutes on 400f/200C, turning once halfway through cooking and spraying with more oil.

5 Ensure the chicken is cooked through and piping hot before serving.

LEMON CHICKEN WINGS

Serves 4

INGREDIENTS

- 12 chicken wings
- 1 tsp olive oil
- 60ml/¼ cup lemon juice
- 60ml/¼ cup soy sauce
- 2 tsp garlic powder
- Low calorie spray oil

NUTRITION

- Calories: 356
- Protein: 29g
- Total Fat: 25g
- Saturated Fat: 8g
- Carbs: 3g
- Fibre: 0g
- Sugars: 0.25g

METHOD

1 Combine together the oil, lemon juice, soy sauce & garlic powder to make a sauce.

2 Place in a plastic bag with the chicken wings and leave to marinate for a few hours (or overnight) in the fridge, turning occasionally to coat the chicken well.

3 Spray well with oil and place in the air fryer basket. Cook for approx. 25-30 minutes on 400f/200C, turning once halfway through cooking and spraying with more oil.

4 Ensure the chicken is cooked through and piping hot before serving.

DRUMSTICKS WORK TOO

MOZZARELLA CHICKEN

Serves 4

INGREDIENTS

- 4 small skinless chicken breasts
- 4 thick slices mozzarella cheese
- 2 tbsp sundried tomato puree/paste
- 125g/4oz plain flour
- 100g/3oz panko breadcrumbs
- 2 eggs
- 4 slices Parma ham
- Wooden cocktail sticks
- Low calorie spray oil

NUTRITION

- Calories: 558
- Protein: 54g
- Total Fat: 16g
- Saturated Fat: 7g
- Carbs: 46g
- Fibre: 3g
- Sugars: 3g

METHOD

1 Butterfly each breast so that it opens out to double its size. Spread some of the puree to the inner side of the chicken and lay a slice of mozzarella inside. Close the breast over back to its original shape (basically you are sandwiching the puree and mozzarella slice in the centre of the chicken).

2 Put the flour on a plate. Place the breadcrumbs in a shallow dish, lay some baking parchment on a plate on the worktop and beat the eggs in a shallow bowl.

3 Gently roll the breasts in the flour. Keeping them closed over so that filling stays hidden in the centre.

4 Dip each breast into the beaten egg and roll it in the breadcrumbs. Again keeping the breast in tact. Lay each slice of Parma ham on the parchment and place the breast on top of each slice. Wrap the breast in the Parma slice and use the cocktail stick to hold it together.

5 Spray well with oil and place in the air fryer basket. Cook for approx. 30-35 minutes on 400f/200C. Turn once halfway through cooking and spray with a little more oil. Ensure the chicken is cooked through and piping hot before serving

6 Give each breast plenty of room in the basket and cook in batches if necessary.

CHICKEN PUFF TARTS

Serves 4

INGREDIENTS

- 2 sheets low fat frozen puff pastry, defrosted
- 2 tbsp tomato puree/paste
- 125g/4oz cooked shredded chicken
- 1 tbsp olive oil
- 75g/3oz spinach, chopped
- 60g/2oz low fat grated cheddar cheese
- Low calorie spray oil

NUTRITION

- Calories: 495
- Protein: 26g
- Total Fat: 24g
- Saturated Fat: 11g
- Carbs: 43g
- Fibre: 3g
- Sugars: 5g

METHOD

1 Cut each sheet of puff pastry in two to make 4 bases.

2 Combine together the tomato puree, chicken, olive oil, spinach & cheese.

3 Divide this mixture into 4 and dollop in the centre of each base.

4 Spray each tart well with oil and place in the air fryer basket.

5 Cook for approx. 6-12 minutes on 400f/200C.

6 Don't put too many tarts in at a time. Give them plenty of room in the basket and cook in batches if necessary.

MARRAKECH CHICKEN GOUJONS & DIP

Serves 4

INGREDIENTS

- 4 skinless chicken breasts
- 1 tbsp plain flour
- 2 tbsp Ras el honout spice mix
- 100g/3oz panko breadcrumbs
- 2 eggs, beaten
- Low calorie spray oil
- 250ml/1 cup low fat natural Greek yoghurt
- 4 tbsp chopped fresh chives & coriander
- 2-3 tsp lemon juice

NUTRITION

- Calories: 349
- Protein: 43g
- Total Fat: 7g
- Saturated Fat: 2g
- Carbs: 26g
- Fibre: 1.5g
- Sugars: 4g

METHOD

1 Cut the chicken into thick finger size strips.

2 Add the flour and 2 tbsp Ras el honout to a plastic bag.

3 Place the breadcrumbs in a shallow dish and lay some baking parchment on a plate on the worktop.

4 Add the chicken strips to the plastic bag and shake well to fully coat.

5 Dip each strip into the beaten egg then roll it in the panko breadcrumbs and place on the baking parchment.

6 Spray each strip well with oil and place in the air fryer basket.

7 Cook for approx. 15 minutes on 400f/200C, turning once halfway through cooking.

8 Don't put too many strips in at a time. Give them plenty of room in the basket and cook in batches if necessary.

9 Whilst the chicken is cooking prepare the dip by combining together the yoghurt, chopped herbs and lemon juice.

SLICED 'FRIED' HOG

Serves 4

INGREDIENTS

- 1kg/2¼lb pork tenderloin
- 2 tbsp maple syrup
- 120ml/½ cup ketchup
- 120ml/½ cup water
- ½ tsp salt
- 120ml/½ cup white vinegar
- 1 tsp soy sauce
- 2 cloves garlic, crushed
- Low calorie spray oil

NUTRITION

- Calories: 422
- Protein: 56g
- Total Fat: 10g
- Saturated Fat: 3g
- Carbs: 22g
- Fibre: 0g
- Sugars: 12g

METHOD

1 Combine together the maple syrup, ketchup, water, salt, vinegar, soy and garlic together to make a sauce.

2 Place the sauce & pork in a large plastic bag and leave to marinate for a few hours (or overnight) in the fridge, turning occasionally to coat the tenderloin well.

3 Spray well with oil and place in the air fryer basket.

4 Cook for approx. 35-45 minutes on 375f/190C, turning once halfway through cooking and spraying with more oil.

5 Ensure the pork is cooked through and piping hot before serving. Thickly slice and serve.

MOZZARELLA BEEF BURGERS

Serves 4

INGREDIENTS

- 125g/4oz ball of low fat mozzarella
- 1 onion, finely chopped
- 2 tsp dried mixed herbs
- 125g/4oz breadcrumbs
- 1 egg, beaten
- 600g/1lb 5oz lean minced beef
- Low calorie spray oil

NUTRITION

- Calories: 428
- Protein: 41g
- Total Fat: 14g
- Saturated Fat: 6g
- Carbs: 28g
- Fibre: 2g
- Sugars: 3g

METHOD

1 First cut the mozzarella ball into 4 even pieces.

2 In a large bowl combine together the chopped onion, herbs, breadcrumbs, egg & minced beef.

3 Shape the mince into a burger around a piece of mozzarella so that the cheese is hidden in the centre of the burger.

4 Spray each burger well with oil and place in the air fryer basket.

5 Cook for approx. 15-20 minutes on 375f/190C, turning once halfway through cooking and spraying with more oil.

6 Ensure the burgers are cooked through and piping hot before serving.

SPANISH STUFFED PORK TENDERLOIN

Serves 4

INGREDIENTS

- 1kg/2¼lb pork tenderloin
- 3 cloves garlic, crushed
- 60g/2oz chopped chorizo
- 150g/5oz spinach, chopped
- 60g/2oz low fat grated Cheddar cheese
- 1 tbsp olive oil
- Low calorie spray oil

NUTRITION

- Calories: 515
- Protein: 66g
- Total Fat: 21g
- Saturated Fat: 7g
- Carbs: 3g
- Fibre: 1g
- Sugars: 0.25g

METHOD

1 First prepare the tenderloin by cutting lengthwise through the centre of the meat. Don't cut it all the way through, just enough so that you can open it out like a book (ie butterfly it).

2 Cover with cling film and give it a good bash to flatten out.

3 Combine together the garlic, chorizo, spinach, cheese & oil and spread this over one side of the butterflied pork.

4 Roll the pork and tie with kitchen string to keep it together.

5 Spray well with oil and place in the air fryer basket.

6 Cook for approx. 35-45 minutes on 375f/190C, turning once halfway through cooking and spraying with more oil.

7 Ensure the pork is cooked through and piping hot before serving. Thickly slice and serve.

MUSTARD STUFFED SAUSAGES

Serves 4

INGREDIENTS

- 8 thick chicken sausages
- 2 tbsp wholegrain mustard
- 1 tbsp ketchup
- 75g/3oz cubed pancetta, finely chopped
- 4 slices back bacon
- Low calorie spray oil
- Cocktail sticks

NUTRITION

- Calories: 409
- Protein: 38g
- Total Fat: 28g
- Saturated Fat: 9g
- Carbs: 2g
- Fibre: 0.5g
- Sugars: 1.25g

METHOD

1 First prepare the sausages by cutting lengthwise through the centre of each. Don't slice all the way through, just enough so that you can open out like a book.

2 Combine together the mustard and ketchup and spread this on the inside of the sausages. Sprinkle the pancetta inside too and wrap each sausage tightly with bacon.

3 Hold in place with a cocktail stick. Spray each sausage well with oil and place in the air fryer basket.

4 Cook for approx. 10-15 minutes on 375f/190C, turning once halfway through cooking and spraying with more oil.

5 Ensure the sausages are cooked through and piping hot before serving.

CRACKED PEPPER STEAK

Serves 1

INGREDIENTS

- 125g/4oz sirloin steak
- 2 tsp olive oil
- 1 tbsp ground black pepper
- Low calorie spray oil
- 120ml/½ cup red wine
- 1 tbsp butter

NUTRITION

- Calories: 487
- Protein: 18g
- Total Fat: 35g
- Saturated Fat: 13g
- Carbs: 6g
- Fibre: 2g
- Sugars: 1g

METHOD

1 Brush the steak with olive oil and press the ground black pepper firmly into both sides of the steak to create a pepper crust.

2 Spray well with oil and place in the air fryer basket.

3 Cook for approx. 8-12 minutes on 400f/200C, turning once halfway through cooking and spraying with more oil.

4 Whilst the steak is cooking gently melt the butter in a saucepan and whisk in the red wine.

5 Ensure the steak is cooked to your taste and serve with the wine sauce poured over the top.

HONEY MUSTARD PORK CHOPS

Serves 4

INGREDIENTS

- 1 tsp English mustard powder
- 1 garlic clove, crushed
- 1 tbsp olive oil
- 2 tbsp honey
- 4 bone in pork chops
- Low calorie spray oil

NUTRITION

- Calories: 282
- Protein: 24g
- Total Fat: 15.5g
- Saturated Fat: 5g
- Carbs: 9g
- Fibre: 0g
- Sugars: 8.5g

METHOD

1 Combine together the mustard powder, garlic, olive oil & honey to make a glaze.

2 Brush the steak liberally with the glaze. Spray well with oil and place in the air fryer basket.

3 Cook for approx. 12-15 minutes on 375f/190C, turning once halfway through cooking and spraying with more oil.

4 Don't put too many chops in at a time. Give them plenty of room in the basket and cook in batches if necessary. Ensure they are cooked through and piping hot.

LAMB KOFTA

Serves 4

INGREDIENTS

- 650g/1lb 7oz lean lamb mince
- 2 tsp ground cumin
- 2 tsp ground coriander
- 2 garlic cloves, crushed
- 1 onion, finely chopped
- 1 tbsp freshly chopped mint
- 1 tbsp olive oil
- Metal skewers
- Low calorie spray oil

NUTRITION

- Calories: 411
- Protein: 29g
- Total Fat: 21g
- Saturated Fat: 8g
- Carbs: 5g
- Fibre: 1g
- Sugars: 2g

METHOD

1 In a large bowl combine together all the ingredients. Divide the mixture into 8 balls and roll into oval shapes.

2 Slide two of these ovals onto a skewer and repeat until you have 4 filled skewers.

3 Spray each kofta well with oil and place in the air fryer basket.

4 Cook for approx. 8-12 minutes on 400f/200C, turning once halfway through cooking and spraying with more oil.

5 Don't put too many in at a time. Give them plenty of room in the basket and cook in batches if necessary. Ensure the kofta are cooked through and piping hot before serving.

ROSEMARY LAMB CHOPS

Serves 4

INGREDIENTS

- 2 garlic cloves, crushed
- 1 tbsp freshly chopped rosemary
- 1 tsp crushed sea salt flakes
- 1 tbsp olive oil
- 4 bone-in lamb chops
- Low calorie spray oil

NUTRITION

- Calories: 303
- Protein: 25.5g
- Total Fat: 22.25g
- Saturated Fat: 8g
- Carbs: 0.5g
- Fibre: 0g
- Sugars: 0g

METHOD

1 Combine together the garlic, rosemary, salt & olive oil.

2 Brush the chops with this garlic oil steak. Spray well with oil and place in the air fryer basket.

3 Cook for approx. 12-15 minutes on 375f/190C, turning once halfway through cooking and spraying with more oil.

4 Don't put too many chops in at a time. Give them plenty of room in the basket and cook in batches if necessary. Ensure they are cooked through and piping hot.

MAIN COURSES FISH & SEAFOOD

TUNA CROQUETTES

Serves 4

INGREDIENTS

- 1 large potato
- Knob of butter
- 1 tbsp chopped chives
- 1 tsp lemon juice
- 4 spring onions, finely chopped
- 1 egg, beaten
- 3 tbsp plain flour
- ½ tsp salt
- 200g/7oz tinned tuna
- 200g/7oz breadcrumbs
- Low calorie spray oil

NUTRITION

- Calories: 358
- Protein: 22g
- Total Fat: 6g
- Saturated Fat: 3g
- Carbs: 56g
- Fibre: 4g
- Sugars: 3g

METHOD

1 Peel, dice and steam the potato until tender.

2 When the potato is tender, gently mash with the back of a fork along with the butter and allow to cool for a few minutes.

3 Combine the potatoes with the chives, lemon juice, onions, egg, flour, salt & tuna. Use your hands to shape the mixture into croquette rolls or balls – use about 2 tbsp of mixture for each.

4 Roll the croquettes in the breadcrumbs until completely coated.

5 Spray with oil and place in the air fryer basket.

6 Cook for approx. 10-14 minutes on 400f/200C. Turn once halfway through cooking and spray with additional oil.

7 Don't put too many in at a time. Give the croquettes plenty of room in the basket and cook in batches if necessary.

DUSTED LEMON SOLE FILLETS

Serves 4

INGREDIENTS

- 75g/3oz self raising flour
- 1 tsp ground black pepper
- 1 tbsp garlic powder
- 2 tsp salt
- 4 skinless boneless lemon sole fillets
- 2 eggs, beaten
- Low calorie spray oil

NUTRITION

- Calories: 247
- Protein: 35g
- Total Fat: 4g
- Saturated Fat: 1g
- Carbs: 17g
- Fibre: 1g
- Sugars: 1g

METHOD

1 Add the flour, pepper, garlic powder & salt to a plastic bag.

2 Brush the fish fillets with the beaten eggs and add to the flour bag.

3 Gently shake to fully coat and place on a tray with some baking parchment.

4 Spray each fillet well with oil and place in the air fryer basket.

5 Cook for approx. 10-15 minutes on 400f/200C, turning once halfway through cooking and spraying with a little more oil.

6 Cook in batches to allow plenty of space in the basket. Ensure the fish is cooked through and piping hot.

TORTILLA FRIED FISH

Serves 4

INGREDIENTS

- 2 pieces of white bread
- 50g/2oz cheesy tortilla chips
- 4 skinless boneless cod fillets
- 2 eggs, beaten
- Low calorie spray oil

NUTRITION

- Calories: 258
- Protein: 33g
- Total Fat: 8g
- Saturated Fat: 2g
- Carbs: 15g
- Fibre: 1g
- Sugars: 1g

ADD FRIES

METHOD

1 In a food processor whizz together the bread & tortilla chips to make breadcrumbs and add this to a plastic bag.

2 Brush the fish fillets with the beaten eggs and add to the bag. Gently shake to fully coat and place on a tray with some baking parchment.

3 Spray each fillet well with oil and place in the air fryer basket.

4 Cook for approx. 10-15 minutes on 400f/200C, turning once halfway through cooking and spraying with a little more oil.

5 Cook in batches to allow plenty of space in the basket. Ensure the fish is cooked through and piping hot.

SWEET CHILLI SALMON

Serves 4

INGREDIENTS

- 2 tbsp reduced sugar sweet chilli sauce
- 1 tbsp soy sauce
- 1 tbsp finely chopped fresh ginger
- 1 tbsp olive oil
- 4 thick skinless boneless salmon fillets
- Low calorie spray oil

NUTRITION

- Calories: 343
- Protein: 35g
- Total Fat: 24g
- Saturated Fat: 4g
- Carbs: 2.5g
- Fibre: 0g
- Sugars: 1.5g

METHOD

1 Combine together the chilli sauce, soy, ginger and olive oil to make a syrupy glaze.

2 Brush the salmon all over with the glaze.

3 Spray each fillet well with oil and place in the air fryer basket.

4 Cook for approx. 8-10 minutes on 400f/200C, turning once halfway through cooking and spraying with a little more oil.

5 Cook in batches to allow plenty of space in the basket. Ensure the salmon is cooked through and piping hot.

THAI CRAB CAKES

Serves 4

INGREDIENTS

- 150g/5oz panko breadcrumbs
- 1 stalk lemongrass, finely chopped
- 75g/3oz green beans, finely chopped
- 200g fresh white crabmeat
- 1 red chilli, de-seeded & finely chopped
- 1 garlic clove, crushed
- 1 tbsp fish sauce
- 1 egg
- 4 spring onions, finely chopped
- 1 tbsp freshly grated ginger
- Handful of fresh coriander stalks
- Low calorie spray oil

NUTRITION

- Calories: 219
- Protein: 16g
- Total Fat: 3g
- Saturated Fat: 1g
- Carbs: 31g
- Fibre: 3g
- Sugars: 3g

METHOD

1 Tip the breadcrumbs onto a plate.

2 In a food processor pulse together the lemon grass, green beans, crabmeat, chilli, garlic, fish sauce, egg, spring onions, ginger & coriander.

3 Form 8 small fishcakes from the mixture and push them gently into the breadcrumbs until completely coated.

4 Spray with oil and place in the air fryer basket.

5 Cook for approx. 10-14 minutes on 375f/190C. Turn once halfway through cooking and spray with additional oil.

6 Don't put too many in at a time. Give the crab cakes plenty of room in the basket and cook in batches if necessary.

BALSAMIC TUNA STEAKS

Serves 4

INGREDIENTS

- 2 tbsp balsamic vinegar
- 1 tsp brown sugar
- 1 tbsp finely chopped oregano
- 1 tbsp olive oil
- 4 thick tuna steaks
- Low calorie spray oil

NUTRITION

- Calories: 316
- Protein: 35g
- Total Fat: 11g
- Saturated Fat: 3g
- Carbs: 2g
- Fibre: 0g
- Sugars: 2g

METHOD

1 Combine together the vinegar, sugar, oregano & olive oil to make a glaze.

2 Brush the tuna all over with the glaze.

3 Spray each steak well with oil and place in the air fryer basket.

4 Cook for approx. 6-8 minutes on 400f/200C, turning once halfway through cooking and spray with a little more oil.

5 Cook in batches in needed to allow plenty of space in the basket. Ensure the tuna is cooked to your liking.

CRAB ROLLS

Serves 4

INGREDIENTS

- 450g/1lb crab meat
- 2 tbsp freshly chopped coriander
- 1 tsp sesame oil
- 1 tsp soy sauce
- 2 spring onions, finely chopped
- 2 tbsp mayonnaise
- 50g/2oz beansprouts
- 1 carrot, peeled & grated
- 16-20 spring roll wrappers
- Low calorie spray oil

NUTRITION

- Calories: 404
- Protein: 27g
- Total Fat: 9g
- Saturated Fat: 2g
- Carbs: 53g
- Fibre: 3g
- Sugars: 3g

METHOD

1 In a food processor pulse together the crab meat, coriander, sesame oil, soy sauce, spring onions, mayonnaise, beansprouts & carrots to create the filling for the rolls.

2 Place a spoonful of filling in the centre of each spring roll wrapper. Bring the bottom edge of the wrapper tightly over the filling, folding in the sides. Continue rolling until the top of the wrapper is reached.

3 Brush the edges of the wrapper with water, pressing to seal. Repeat until all the wrappers are used. (You'll need to experiment with how much mixture to ensure you don't overfill or under-fill the rolls).

4 Spray each roll well with oil and place in the air fryer basket.

5 Cook for approx. 8-10 minutes on 400f/200C. Turn once halfway through cooking and spray with additional oil.

6 Don't put too many rolls in at a time. Give them plenty of room in the basket and cook in batches of 4 if necessary.

MAIN COURSES VEGETABLE

FETA FILO PIES

Serves 4

INGREDIENTS

- 1 egg yolk
- 150g/5oz low fat feta cheese
- 2 tbsp freshly chopped flat leaf parsley
- Small bunch spring onions, finely chopped
- Ground black pepper to taste
- 2 sheets low fat frozen filo pastry, defrosted
- Low calorie spray oil

NUTRITION

- Calories: 148
- Protein: 9g
- Total Fat: 6g
- Saturated Fat: 3g
- Carbs: 16g
- Fibre: 1g
- Sugars: 4g

METHOD

1 Beat the egg yolk in a bowl and mix in the feta, parsley and spring onions. Season with pepper to taste.

2 Cut each sheet of filo pastry into three strips. Scoop a spoonful of the feta mixture onto each strip of pastry. Fold the tip of the pastry over the filling to form a triangle. Fold the strips criss-crossed until the filling is wrapped in a pastry triangle. Repeat until all the pastry and feta has been used.

3 Spray each pie well with oil and place in the air fryer basket.

4 Cook for approx. 12-15 minutes on 350f/175C. Turn once halfway through cooking and spray with additional oil.

5 Don't put too many pies in at a time. Give them plenty of room in the basket and cook in batches if necessary.

PESTO & TOMATO TARTS

Serves 4

INGREDIENTS

- 2 tbsp low fat green pesto
- 125g/4oz cherry tomato, halved
- 125g/4oz grated low fat cheddar cheese
- 2 sheets low fat frozen puff pastry, defrosted
- Low calorie spray oil

NUTRITION

- Calories: 295
- Protein: 12g
- Total Fat: 17g
- Saturated Fat: 7g
- Carbs: 23g
- Fibre: 1g
- Sugars: 3g

METHOD

1 Cut each sheet of puff pastry in two to make 4 bases.

2 Dot the pesto in the centre of each base and spread to cover most of the base. Add some cherry tomato halves and sprinkle with cheese.

3 Spray each tart well with oil and place in the air fryer basket.

4 Cook for approx. 6-12 minutes on 400f/200C.

5 Don't put too many tarts in at a time. Give them plenty of room in the basket and cook in batches if necessary.

QUICK & EASY

PINE NUT TOPPED TOMATOES

Serves 4

INGREDIENTS

- 2 tbsp pine nuts, finely chopped
- 2 tbsp breadcrumbs
- 2 tbsp freshly chopped flat leaf parsley
- 2 tsp grated Parmesan cheese
- 1 garlic clove, crushed
- 1 tsp olive oil
- 4 large beef tomatoes, halved
- Low calorie spray oil

NUTRITION

- Calories: 96
- Protein: 3g
- Total Fat: 5g
- Saturated Fat: 1g
- Carbs: 12g
- Fibre: 3g
- Sugars: 6g

METHOD

1 Combine together the pine nuts, breadcrumbs, parsley, cheese, garlic and olive oil.

2 Sit the beef tomatoes centre side up and pile on the pine nut topping.

3 Spray each tomato well with oil and place in the air fryer basket.

4 Cook for approx. 8-12 minutes on 375f/190C.

5 Don't put too many tomatoes in at a time. Give them plenty of room in the basket and cook in batches if necessary.

RICOTTA STUFFED MUSHROOMS

Serves 4

INGREDIENTS

- 75g/3oz low fat halloumi cheese, finely diced
- 75g/3oz breadcrumbs
- 150g/5oz low fat ricotta cheese
- 4 tbsp low fat pesto
- 4 large portabella mushrooms
- Low calorie spray oil

NUTRITION

- Calories: 245
- Protein: 13g
- Total Fat: 10g
- Saturated Fat: 4g
- Carbs: 24g
- Fibre: 3g
- Sugars: 6g

METHOD

1 Combine together the halloumi cheese, breadcrumbs, ricotta and pesto.

2 Sit the mushrooms flat side up and arrange the pesto mixture over the top of each mushroom.

3 Spray each mushroom well with oil and place in the air fryer basket.

4 Cook for approx. 10-12 minutes on 400f/200C and spray with additional oil half way through cooking.

5 Don't put too many mushrooms in at a time. Give them plenty of room in the basket and cook in batches if necessary.

AUBERGINE CIABATTA

Serves 4

INGREDIENTS

- 3 large aubergines
- Crushed sea salt flakes
- Ground black pepper
- 4 ciabatta rolls
- Low calorie spray oil
- 1 tbsp mayonnaise
- 1 tbsp garlic olive oil (optional)

NUTRITION

- Calories: 358
- Protein: 10g
- Total Fat: 6g
- Saturated Fat: 1g
- Carbs: 65g
- Fibre: 9g
- Sugars: 10g

METHOD

1 Split the aubergines in half lengthways and season the exposed flesh with the salt and pepper.

2 Spray with oil and cook for approx. 15-20 minutes on 400f/200C and spray with additional oil half way through cooking.

3 Don't put too many aubergines in at a time. Give them plenty of room in the basket and cook in batches if necessary.

4 Meanwhile split the ciabatta rolls in half and lightly toast.

5 When the aubergines are tender separate the flesh from the skins with a fork (this should come away easily). Add a little more seasoning along with the mayonnaise and pile onto the toasted ciabatta.

6 Drizzle with garlic oil (if using) and serve.

VEGETABLE SIDES

FRIED GARLIC ASPARAGUS

Serves 4

INGREDIENTS

- 400g/14oz fresh asparagus tips
- 3 tbsp cornstarch
- 1 tsp salt
- 200g/7oz breadcrumbs
- 1 tbsp mixed dried herbs
- 2 tsp garlic powder
- 2 eggs
- Low calorie spray oil

NUTRITION

- Calories: 282
- Protein: 11g
- Total Fat: 5g
- Saturated Fat: 1g
- Carbs: 49g
- Fibre: 5g
- Sugars: 5g

METHOD

1 Add the cornstarch and salt to a plastic bag.

2 Combine together the breadcrumbs, herbs and garlic powder in bowl.

3 Beat the eggs together in a separate bowl

4 Lay some baking parchment on a plate on the worktop.

5 Add the asparagus spears to the cornstarch and shake well to fully coat.

6 Dip each spear into the beaten egg then roll it in the breadcrumbs and place on the baking parchment.

7 Spray each spear well with oil and place in the air fryer basket.

8 Cook for approx. 6-8 minutes on 400f/200C. Turn once halfway through cooking and spray with additional oil.

9 Don't put too many spears in at a time. Give them plenty of room in the basket and cook in batches if necessary.

NUTMEG ROASTED TURNIP

Serves 4

INGREDIENTS

- 2 turnips
- 1 tsp ground nutmeg
- 1 tsp salt
- 3 tbsp cornstarch
- Low calorie spray oil

NUTRITION

- Calories: 43
- Protein: 0.5g
- Total Fat: 0.25g
- Saturated Fat: 0g
- Carbs: 10g
- Fibre: 2g
- Sugars: 3g

METHOD

1 Peel and cube the turnips. Pat dry with kitchen towels.

2 Combine the cornstarch, nutmeg and salt in a plastic bag. Add the turnip to the cornstarch and shake well to fully coat the cubes.

3 Spray each cube well with oil and place in the air fryer basket.

4 Cook for approx. 25-35 minutes on 375f/190C.

5 Open up the fryer now and again during cooking and give the basket a good shake. Ensure the turnip is tender and cooked through before serving.

PARMESAN MINI CORN

Serves 2

INGREDIENTS

- 2 large cobs of corn
- 1 tbsp butter
- 1 tbsp grated Parmesan cheese
- Low calorie spray oil

NUTRITION

- Calories: 241
- Protein: 6g
- Total Fat: 9g
- Saturated Fat: 5g
- Carbs: 41g
- Fibre: 4g
- Sugars: 7g

METHOD

1 Peel the corn and cut each of the cobs into four pieces.

2 Spray piece well with oil and place in the air fryer basket.

3 Cook for approx. 15-20 minutes on 400f/200C or until tender.

4 Whilst the corn is cooking, gently melt the butter. When the corn is ready brush with butter and sprinkle the grated Parmesan over the top.

TASTY

CRUNCHY COATED SPROUTS

Serves 4

INGREDIENTS

- 400g/14oz Brussels sprouts, peeled
- 3 tbsp cornstarch
- Pinch of salt
- 100g/3oz breadcrumbs
- 2 tbsp grated Parmesan cheese
- 2 eggs
- Low calorie spray oil

NUTRITION

- Calories: 304
- Protein: 12g
- Total Fat: 6g
- Saturated Fat: 2g
- Carbs: 51g
- Fibre: 6g
- Sugars: 5g

METHOD

1 Add the cornstarch and salt to a plastic bag.

2 Combine together the breadcrumbs and Parmesan in bowl.

3 Beat the eggs together in a separate bowl

4 Lay some baking parchment on a plate on the worktop.

5 Add the sprouts to the cornstarch and shake well to fully coat.

6 Dip each sprout into the beaten egg then roll it in the breadcrumbs and place on the baking parchment.

7 Spray each sprout well with oil and place in the air fryer basket.

8 Cook for approx. 15-20 minutes on 350f/175C. Turn once halfway through cooking and spray with additional oil. Ensure they are tender and piping hot before serving.

9 Don't put too many sprouts in at a time. Give them plenty of room in the basket and cook in batches if necessary.

COURGETTE BASIL BUTTONS

Serves 4

INGREDIENTS

- 4 courgettes/zucchini
- 3 tbsp cornstarch
- Pinch of salt
- 100g/3oz panko breadcrumbs
- 1 tbsp dried basil
- 1 tbsp grated Parmesan
- 2 eggs
- Low calorie spray oil

NUTRITION

- Calories: 185
- Protein: 8g
- Total Fat: 4g
- Saturated Fat: 1g
- Carbs: 31g
- Fibre: 4g
- Sugars: 6g

METHOD

1 Slice the courgettes into discs about a 1cm thick.

2 Add the cornstarch and salt to a plastic bag.

3 Combine together the breadcrumbs, basil and Parmesan in bowl.

4 Beat the eggs together in a separate bowl

5 Lay some baking parchment on a plate on the worktop.

6 Add the courgettes to the cornstarch and shake well to fully coat.

7 Dip each button into the beaten egg then roll it in the breadcrumbs and place on the baking parchment. Spray each button well with oil and place in the air fryer basket.

8 Cook for approx. 8-10 minutes on 400f/200C. Turn once halfway through cooking and spray with additional oil.

9 Don't put too many buttons in at a time. Give them plenty of room in the basket and cook in batches if necessary.

SKINNY SWEET POTATO FRIES

Serves 4

INGREDIENTS

- 2 large sweet potatoes
- 1 tbsp olive oil
- 1 tsp crushed sea salt flakes
- Low calorie spray oil

NUTRITION

- Calories: 138
- Protein: 2g
- Total Fat: 4g
- Saturated Fat: 0.5g
- Carbs: 25g
- Fibre: 3g
- Sugars: 5g

METHOD

1 Peel and cut the sweet potatoes into evenly sized skinny fries. Pat dry with some kitchen roll.

2 Combine together the fries, oil & salt to evenly coat the sweet potatoes.

3 Spray the fries with oil and place in the air fryer basket.

4 Cook for approx. 10 minutes on 400f/200C. Turn once halfway through cooking and spray with additional oil.

5 Don't put too many fries in at a time. Give them plenty of room in the basket and cook in batches if necessary. Make sure they are tender inside and crispy outside before serving.

CRUNCHY PARMESAN SWEET POTATO FRIES

Serves 4

INGREDIENTS

- 2 large sweet potatoes
- 1 tbsp grated Parmesan cheese
- 1 tsp garlic powder
- 1 tsp paprika
- Low calorie spray oil

NUTRITION

- Calories: 117
- Protein: 3g
- Total Fat: 1g
- Saturated Fat: 0.3g
- Carbs: 26g
- Fibre: 3g
- Sugars: 5g

METHOD

1 Peel and cut the sweet potatoes into evenly sized skinny fries. Pat dry with some kitchen roll.

2 Combine together the fries, grated cheese, garlic powder & paprika to evenly coat the sweet potatoes.

3 Spray the fries with oil and place in the air fryer basket.

4 Cook for approx. 10 minutes on 400f/200C. Turn once halfway through cooking and spray with additional oil.

5 Don't put too many fries in at a time. Give them plenty of room in the basket and cook in batches if necessary. Make sure they are tender inside and crispy outside before serving.

SWEET POTATO COCONUT DUMPLINGS

Serves 4

INGREDIENTS

- 2 large sweet potatoes
- 2 tbsp coconut powder
- 2 tsp olive oil
- 125g/4oz glutinous rice flour
- 50g/2oz brown sugar
- Low calorie spray oil

NUTRITION

- Calories: 422
- Protein: 5g
- Total Fat: 5g
- Saturated Fat: 2g
- Carbs: 90g
- Fibre: 4g
- Sugars: 18g

METHOD

1 Peel, dice and steam the sweet potatoes.

2 When the sweet potato is tender, gently mash with the back of a fork.

3 In a bowl combine together the cooked potato, coconut powder, olive oil and brown sugar until it comes together as an even dough.

4 Divide the dough and roll into small balls (about a tablespoon of dough for each dumpling).

5 Spray the dumplings with oil and place in the air fryer basket.

6 Cook for approx. 10-14 minutes on 375f/190C. Turn once halfway through cooking and spray with additional oil.

7 Don't put too many dumplings in at a time. Give them plenty of room in the basket and cook in batches if necessary. Make sure they are tender inside and crispy outside before serving.

SWEET PARMENTIER

Serves 4

INGREDIENTS

- 2 large sweet potatoes
- 1 tbsp olive oil
- 2 tsp garlic powder
- 1 tsp dried mixed herbs
- Low calorie spray oil

NUTRITION

- Calories: 143
- Protein: 2g
- Total Fat: 4g
- Saturated Fat: 0.5g
- Carbs: 27g
- Fibre: 3g
- Sugars: 5g

METHOD

1 Peel and cube the sweet potatoes into small 2cm cubes. Pat dry with some kitchen roll.

2 In a bowl combine together the cubes, olive oil, garlic powder & herbs to evenly coat the sweet potatoes.

3 Spray the cubes with oil and place in the air fryer basket.

4 Cook for approx. 10-20 minutes on 375f/190C. Turn once halfway through cooking and spray with additional oil.

5 Don't put too many potatoes in at a time. Give them plenty of room in the basket and cook in batches if necessary. Make sure they are tender inside and crispy outside before serving.

TRY BUTTERNUT SQUASH

ROAST SALAD POTATOES

Serves 4

INGREDIENTS

- 400g/4oz small salad potatoes
- 1 tsp crushed sea salt flakes
- Low calorie spray oil

NUTRITION

- Calories: 80
- Protein: 2g
- Total Fat: 0.25g
- Saturated Fat: 0g
- Carbs: 18g
- Fibre: 3g
- Sugars: 2g

METHOD

1 Leave the skins on the salad potatoes.

2 Give each potato a good spay with oil and sprinkle with salt.

3 Cook for approx. 30-40 minutes on 375f/190C. Give the potatoes a shake now and again during cooking and spray with a little more oil.

4 Don't put too many potatoes in at a time. Give them plenty of room in the basket and cook in batches if necessary. Make sure they are tender inside and crispy outside before serving.

ADD YOUR FAVOURITE HERBS

CHIPS, CHIPS, CHIPS!

Serves 4

INGREDIENTS

- 2 large potatoes
- 1 tbsp olive oil
- Low calorie spray oil

NUTRITION

- Calories: 147
- Protein: 3g
- Total Fat: 3.5g
- Saturated Fat: 0.5g
- Carbs: 27g
- Fibre: 3g
- Sugars: 1.5g

METHOD

1 Peel and cut the potatoes into evenly sized skinny fries.

2 Place in a bowl of cold water and leave to soak for 30 minutes. Drain and pat dry with some kitchen roll.

3 Combine together the fries & oil to evenly coat the fries.

4 Cook for approx. 15-20 minutes on 375f/190C. Turn once halfway through cooking and spray with oil.

5 Don't put too many fries in at a time. Give them plenty of room in the basket and cook in batches if necessary. Make sure they are tender inside and crispy outside before serving.

SERVE WITH MAYO

HERBED WEDGES

Serves 4

INGREDIENTS

- 2 large potatoes
- 1 tbsp olive oil
- 1 tbsp dried mixed herbs
- 1 tsp paprika
- Low calorie spray oil

NUTRITION

- Calories: 152
- Protein: 3g
- Total Fat: 3.6g
- Saturated Fat: 0.5g
- Carbs: 28g
- Fibre: 4g
- Sugars: 1.5g

METHOD

1 Cut the potatoes into wedges. Place in a bowl of cold water and leave to soak for 30 minutes. Drain and pat dry with some kitchen roll.

2 Combine together the fries, oil, herbs and paprika to evenly coat the wedges.

3 Cook for approx. 20-30 minutes on 350f/180C. Turn once halfway through cooking and spray with oil.

4 Don't put too many wedges in at a time. Give them plenty of room in the basket and cook in batches if necessary. Make sure they are tender inside and crispy outside before serving.

PATATAS BRAVAS

Serves 4

INGREDIENTS

- 2 large potatoes
- 4 tbsp olive oil
- 1 tsp paprika
- Low calorie spray oil
- 1 small onion, chopped
- 2 garlic cloves, crushed
- 200g/7oz tinned tomatoes
- 1 tbsp tomato purée/paste
- 1 tsp chilli powder
- ½ tsp sugar

NUTRITION

- Calories: 264
- Protein: 4.5g
- Total Fat: 14g
- Saturated Fat: 2g
- Carbs: 35g
- Fibre: 5g
- Sugars: 5g

METHOD

1 Peel and cube the potatoes into small 2cm cubes.

2 Place in a bowl of cold water and leave to soak for 30 minutes. Drain and pat dry with some kitchen roll.

3 Combine together the cubes with 1 tbsp of the oil and paprika to evenly coat the cubes.

4 Spray the cubes with oil and place in the air fryer basket.

5 Cook for approx. 10-20 minutes on 375f/190C. Give the basket a good shake now and again during cooking and spray with additional oil.

6 Don't put too many potatoes in at a time. Give them plenty of room in the basket and cook in batches if necessary. Make sure they are tender inside and crispy outside.

7 Meanwhile gently sauté the onion in the rest of the olive oil for a few minutes until softened. Add the garlic, tomatoes, purée, chilli powder, sugar & salt and bring to the boil. Reduce the heat and leave to gently simmer for approx. 10 minutes. Serve over the top of the fried potatoes.

BROCCOLI & POTATO CROQUETTES

Serves 4

INGREDIENTS

- 2 large potatoes
- 1 small head broccoli, chopped
- Knob of butter
- 1 egg, beaten
- 3 tbsp plain flour
- ½ tsp salt
- 100g/3oz breadcrumbs
- Low calorie spray oil

NUTRITION

- Calories: 287
- Protein: 10g
- Total Fat: 5g
- Saturated Fat: 2.4g
- Carbs: 52g
- Fibre: 6g
- Sugars: 4g

METHOD

1 Peel, dice and steam the potatoes until tender. Add the chopped broccoli to the steamer a couple of minutes before the potatoes are ready.

2 When the potato is tender, gently mash with the back of a fork along with the butter and allow to cool for a few minutes.

3 Combine the potatoes with the chopped broccoli, egg, flour and salt. Use your hands to shape the mixture into croquette rolls or balls – use about 2 tbsp of mixture for each.

4 Roll the croquettes in the breadcrumbs until completely coated.

5 Spray with oil and place in the air fryer basket.

6 Cook for approx. 10-14 minutes on 400f/200C. Turn once halfway through cooking and spray with additional oil.

7 Don't put too many in at a time. Give the croquettes plenty of room in the basket and cook in batches if necessary.

SOURED CREAM BAKED POTATOES

Serves 2

INGREDIENTS

- 2 large potatoes
- Low calorie spray oil
- 2 tbsp low fat soured cream
- 1 tbsp chopped chives
- 1 tbsp chopped flat leaf parsley
- 2 tsp Worcestershire sauce
- 1 tsp paprika

NUTRITION

- Calories: 135
- Protein: 3.3g
- Total Fat: 1.5g
- Saturated Fat: 0.8g
- Carbs: 27.8g
- Fibre: 3g
- Sugars: 2g

METHOD

1 Give the potatoes a scrub and pierce with a fork.

2 Spray well with oil and cook for approx. 35-45 minutes on 400f/200C. Turn once halfway through cooking and spray with oil.

3 Meanwhile combine together the sour cream, chives, parsley, Worcestershire sauce & paprika.

4 When the potatoes are cooked through open up and dollop the soured cream on top.

DESSERTS

THE EASIEST APPLE TURNOVERS EVER

Serves 4

INGREDIENTS

- 2 small sheets low fat frozen puff pastry, defrosted
- 4 tbsp apple sauce
- 4 tsp brown sugar
- Low calorie spray oil

NUTRITION

- Calories: 203
- Protein: 3g
- Total Fat: 9g
- Saturated Fat: 4.5g
- Carbs: 27g
- Fibre: 1g
- Sugars: 7g

METHOD

1 Cut each sheet of puff pastry in two to make 4 bases.

2 Dollop a tablespoon of apple sauce in the centre of each base and fold corner to corner to make a triangle. Press all the edges down hard to seal.

3 Spray each triangle with oil and sprinkle the brown sugar over the top. Place in the air fryer basket. Cook for approx. 6-12 minutes on 350f/175C. Turn and spray with more oil halfway through cooking.

4 Don't put too many turnovers in at a time. Give them plenty of room in the basket and cook in batches if necessary.

COOKIE PUFFS

Serves 4

INGREDIENTS

- Small roll of croissant dough (175g/6oz)
- 4 cookies
- Low calorie spray oil

NUTRITION

- Calories: 225
- Protein: 4g
- Total Fat: 13g
- Saturated Fat: 6.5g
- Carbs: 25g
- Fibre: 1g
- Sugars: 8g

METHOD

1 Divide the dough into 4 equal portions.

2 Roll each piece out a little and wrap around a cookie.

3 Spray each cookie puff well with oil and place in the air fryer basket.

4 Cook for approx. 6-10 minutes on 350f/175C. Turn and spray with more oil halfway through cooking.

KIDS TREAT

CHOCOLATE ROTI

Serves 2

INGREDIENTS

- 2 roti (flat bread)
- 2 tbsp hazelnut chocolate spread
- 1 tsp icing sugar
- 1 egg beaten
- Low calorie spray oil

NUTRITION

- Calories: 443
- Protein: 13g
- Total Fat: 13.5g
- Saturated Fat: 2.8g
- Carbs: 69g
- Fibre: 6g
- Sugars: 15g

METHOD

1 Put the roti slices in the freezer for an hour or two to harden.

2 Spread the chocolate all over the top of one and cover with the other roti to make a chocolate 'sandwich'.

3 Brush both sides with the beaten egg and spray with oil

4 Place in the air fryer basket and cook for approx. 5-8 minutes on 375f/190C. Turn and spray with more oil halfway through cooking.

5 Sprinkle with icing sugar and serve.

EASY DESSERT

BANANA GYOZA DUMPLINGS

Serves 2

INGREDIENTS

- 8 gyoza wrappers
- 1 ripe banana, sliced into 8
- 3-4 tbsp hazelnut chocolate spread
- 1 tsp icing sugar
- Low calorie spray oil

NUTRITION

- Calories: 290
- Protein: 4g
- Total Fat: 9g
- Saturated Fat: 1.5g
- Carbs: 50g
- Fibre: 3g
- Sugars: 24g

METHOD

1 Lay the gyoza wrappers out. Place a piece of banana in the centre of each wrapper and dollop a teaspoon or two of chocolate spread on top of each banana slice.

2 Pinch the dumplings edges closed and seal with a little water.

3 Spray with oil, place in the air fryer basket and cook for approx. 3-5 minutes on 400f/200C. Turn and spray with more oil halfway through cooking.

4 Sprinkle with icing sugar and serve.

BLUEBERRY STRUDEL

Serves 2

INGREDIENTS

- 2 small sheets low fat frozen puff pastry, defrosted
- 150g/5oz blueberries (1 pint)
- 1 tbsp brown sugar
- ½ tsp lemon juice
- ½ tsp cornstarch
- 1 egg yolk, beaten
- 2 tsp icing sugar
- Low calorie spray oil

NUTRITION

- Calories: 235
- Protein: 4g
- Total Fat: 10g
- Saturated Fat: 4.9g
- Carbs: 32g
- Fibre: 2g
- Sugars: 10g

METHOD

1 Lay the two sheets of pastry out on some baking parchment.

2 Combine together the blueberries, sugar, cornstarch & lemon juice,

3 Spoon half the blueberry filling onto one half of each pastry square leaving a cm clear around the edges.

4 Brush the edges of the pastry with the egg, fold the half of pastry without filling over the filling and press down the edges to seal.

5 Brush the top with a little more egg. Spray with oil, place in the air fryer basket and cook for approx. 8-12 minutes on 375f/190C. Turn and spray with more oil halfway through cooking. Sprinkle with icing sugar and serve.

CINNAMON PEARS

Serves 4

INGREDIENTS

- 4 large pears
- 3 tbsp brown sugar
- 2 tsp ground cinnamon
- 1 tsp butter
- Low calorie spray oil

NUTRITION

- Calories: 128
- Protein: 0.6g
- Total Fat: 1g
- Saturated Fat: 0.6g
- Carbs: 32g
- Fibre: 6g
- Sugars: 22g

METHOD

1 Split the pears in half lengthways and sprinkle the exposed flesh with sugar, cinnamon and a dot of butter.

2 Spray with oil and cook for approx. 15-20 minutes on 400f/200C and spray with additional oil half way through cooking.

3 Don't put too many pear halves in at a time. Give them plenty of room in the basket and cook in batches if necessary.

TRY WITH APPLES

FRIED PANKO BANANAS

Serves 4

INGREDIENTS

- 4 large bananas, peeled
- 150g/5oz panko breadcrumbs
- 2 tbsp corn flour
- 2 eggs, beaten
- Low calorie spray oil

NUTRITION

- Calories: 297
- Protein: 10g
- Total Fat: 4.5g
- Saturated Fat: 1g
- Carbs: 58g
- Fibre: 4.5g
- Sugars: 22g

METHOD

1 Cut the bananas in half to make 8 pieces.

2 Roll the bananas in the flour, dip them into the eggs and roll in the panko breadcrumbs.

3 Spray each banana half well and place in the air fryer basket.

4 Cook for approx. 5-10 minutes on 350f/175C. Open up the fryer now and again during cooking and give the basket a good shake.

5 Don't put too many bananas in at a time. Give them plenty of room in the basket and cook in batches if necessary.

PERFECT PUDDING